Life Cy

by Steven Danan

PEARSON

Scott
Foresman

DK

How does a frog grow?

A frog starts as an egg.

A tadpole swims out of the egg.

A **tadpole** is a young frog.

The tadpole has a tail.

The tadpole lives in water.

The tadpole grows and changes.

Grown Frog

The tadpole grows into a frog.

The frog lives in water.

The frog lives on land too.

Tadpoles become frogs.
They grow and change.
These changes are called a
life cycle.

How does a butterfly grow?

A butterfly starts as an egg.

A larva comes out of the egg.

A butterfly larva is a caterpillar.

A **larva** is a young insect.

The caterpillar grows.

It makes a hard cover.

It is called a **pupa** as it changes in the cover.

It comes out as a butterfly.

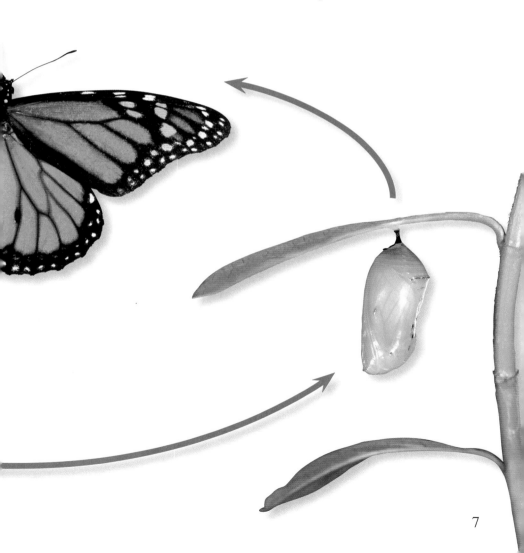

How do animals grow and change?

Young animals change as they grow.

They can change size.

They can change shape.

They can change color.

Growing Up

Young animals grow up.

They can look like their parents.

They can also look different.

How does a daisy grow?

Most plants grow from seeds.

A **seed coat** covers the seed.

It keeps the seed safe.

A seedling grows from the seed.

The **seedling** is a young plant.

A daisy starts as a seed.

Roots, a stem, and flowers grow.

Flowers make seeds.

This is the life cycle of a daisy.

How does a tree grow?

Trees grow from seeds.

Trees change as they grow.

Trees take many years to grow.

How a Cherry Tree Grows

A cherry tree grows fruit.

Cherry trees make cherries.

Cherry trees grow from cherry seeds.

How do plants grow and change?

Flowers have different colors.

Flowers have different shapes.

Flowers have different patterns.

Plants can change as they grow.

Plants and animals have life cycles.
Plants and animals grow and
change.

Glossary

larva
a young insect

life cycle
all the changes of a living thing as it grows

pupa
what the larva may become as it changes into a grown insect

seed coat
a hard cover that protects a seed

seedling
a young plant

tadpole
a young frog